AREA 51

JILL HANEY

red rhino
b**OO**ks®
NONFICTION

Area 51

Cloning

Drones

Fault Lines

Great Spies of the World

Monsters of the Deep

Monsters on Land

Seven Wonders of the
 Ancient World

Virtual Reality

Witchcraft

Wormholes

SADDLEBACK
EDUCATIONAL PUBLISHING
www.sdlback.com

ISBN-13: 978-1-68021-031-6
ISBN-10: 1-68021-031-9
eBook: 978-1-63078-338-9

Printed in Singapore by Craft Print International Ltd
0000/CA00000000

19 18 17 16 15   1 2 3 4 5

TABLE OF CONTENTS

Chapter 1
UFO? 3

Chapter 2
Top Secret 10

Chapter 3
Stay Out 14

Chapter 4
Why So Secret? 20

Chapter 5
Spy Planes 26

Chapter 6
More Secret Projects 30

Chapter 7
Alien Secrets? 34

Chapter 8
Lazar's Story 38

Chapter 9
Spaceships or Spy Planes? 42

Chapter 10
Still a Mystery 46

Glossary 50

Chapter 1
UFO?

It is dark night.

Clouds cover the moon.

Two headlights shine.

It is a car.

Driving down a lonely highway.

A young woman is at the wheel.

Her friend sits next to her.

They talk and laugh.

The radio plays music.

Then the music stops.

There is only *static*.

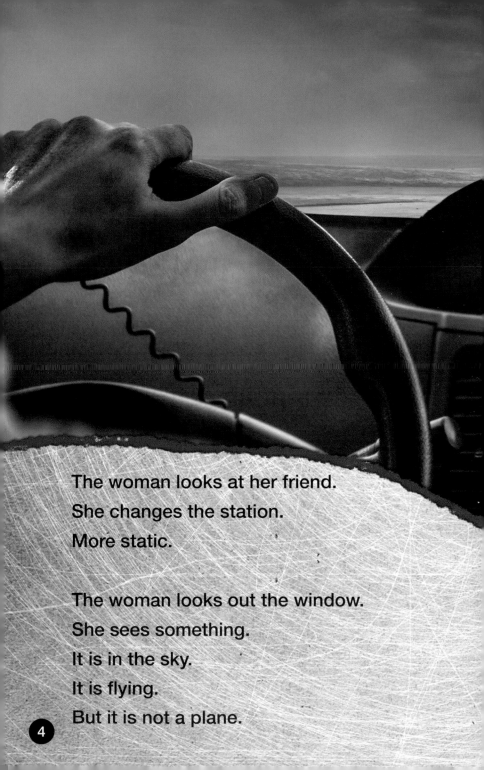

The woman looks at her friend.
She changes the station.
More static.

The woman looks out the window.
She sees something.
It is in the sky.
It is flying.
But it is not a plane.

It looks round.

Like a *disc*.

Red lights blink.

What could it be?

The woman slows down the car.

She pulls the car over.

Her friend sees it too.

Maybe it's a ship.

An *alien* spaceship.

They get out a camera.
But then all is dark.
The flying object is gone.
It has disappeared.
How can that be?

This sounds like a movie.

Or a TV show.

But it's not.

It's a *sighting*.

One of many.

People say they have seen strange
aircraft.
They call them *UFOs*.
Unidentified flying objects.
All in one part of Nevada.
A place called Area 51.

Chapter 2
TOP SECRET

What is Area 51?

It is a top-secret base.

The U.S. *military* uses it.

But they don't talk about it.

Few know what goes on there.

Area 51 is in the desert,

100 miles north of Las Vegas.

It is in the middle of nowhere.

Almost no one lives there.

GROOM LAKE

CAUTION

RADIOACTIVE MATERIALS

DID YOU KNOW?

You can find Area 51 on Google Earth. Type in the coordinates. 37 degrees 14 minutes north latitude. 115 degrees 48 minutes west longitude.

It is near a dried lakebed.

Groom Lake.

Just west is the Nevada Test Site.

Nuclear weapons were tested there.

That began in the 1950s.

It ended 40 years later.

What is at Area 51?

A few buildings.

A *hangar*.

A guard shack.

Places to live. Eat. Work.

And runways.

Planes can land here.

And take off.

Some think there is more.

Secret levels.

Underground.

But no one knows for sure.

WARNING

Restricted Area

It is unlawful to enter this area without
permission of the Installation Commander.
Sec. 21, Internal Security Act of 1950, 50 U.S.C. 797

While on this installation all personnel and
the property under their control are subject
to search.

Use of deadly force authorized.

WARNING!

NO TRESPASSING
AUTHORITY N.R.S. 207-200
MAXIMUM PUNISHMENT: $1000 FINE
SIX MONTHS IMPRISONMENT
OR BOTH
STRICTLY ENFORCED

PHOTOGRAPHY
OF THIS AREA
IS PROHIBITED

18-66-795

WARNING

MILITARY INSTALLATION

IT IS UNLAWFUL TO ENTER THIS INSTALLATION WITHOUT
THE WRITTEN PERMISSION OF THE INSTALLATION COMMANDER.

INSTALLATION COMMANDER
AUTHORITY: Internal Security Act, 50
U.S.C. 797
PUNISHMENT: Up to one year imprisonment
and $5,000. fine.

Chapter 3
STAY OUT

What happens at Area 51 is top secret.

Only a few know.

People work there.

But they can't say what they do.

They sign an *oath*.

Make a promise.

They tell nothing.

If they do, they can go to jail.

Most planes cannot fly over Area 51.
It is against the law.
But planes land there every day.
They carry base workers.
The planes are *unmarked*.
They have special codes.

There are signs around the base.

They say, "Keep Out."

"No Photos."

"No *Trespassing*."

Guards patrol the area.
They usually just watch.
But they have taken people's film.
They don't want photos taken.

There are *sensors* too.
They are buried around the base.
Someone may walk over them.
Then they sound an alarm.

Today, there are photos of Area 51.
They are taken from *satellites*.
You can see them yourself.
But it was not always this way.
Photos were hidden for years.
They were deleted.
The military did not want them seen.

It was the same with maps.
Area 51 was not on maps.
The road to it was left off too.

Chapter 4
WHY SO SECRET?

It takes work to keep a secret.

It is not easy to do.

Area 51 was hidden for years.

Why?

It makes people wonder.

They talk.

Stories get started.

TOP SECRET

Many have guessed about Area 51.
Is it a place for secret *experiments*?
A military prison?
Alien research site?
No one knows.
The truth is hidden.

DID YOU KNOW?

Who chose to test spy planes at Area 51? The CIA and the U.S. Air Force. They liked that it was in the middle of nowhere.

Papers were made public in 2013.
They gave some answers.
They tell about spy planes.
Ones built in the 1950s and 1960s.
Area 51 is where they were tested.

Spy planes.
They are used in war.
They spy on *enemy* countries.
The U.S. would want those secret.
Top secret.
Enemies could not know about them.

Spy planes are useful.
They show what an enemy is doing.
They help win wars.

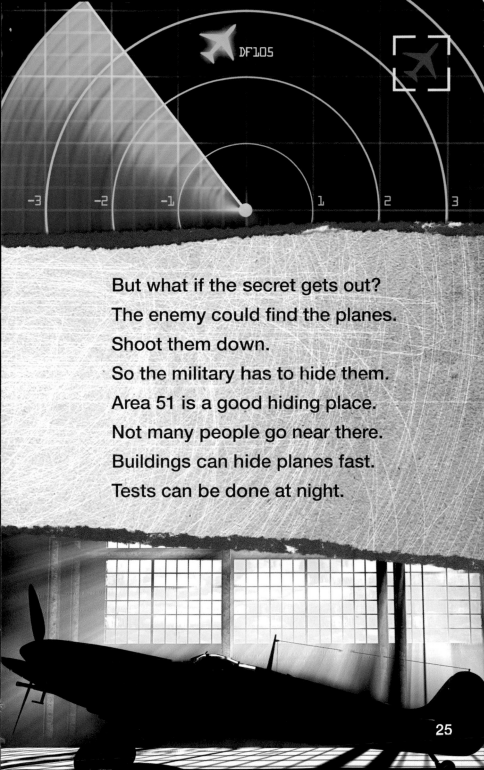

But what if the secret gets out?

The enemy could find the planes.

Shoot them down.

So the military has to hide them.

Area 51 is a good hiding place.

Not many people go near there.

Buildings can hide planes fast.

Tests can be done at night.

Chapter 5
SPY PLANES

It was the 1950s.

The U.S. was at a *standoff*.

It had nuclear weapons.

So did the Soviet Union.

Each country spied on the other.

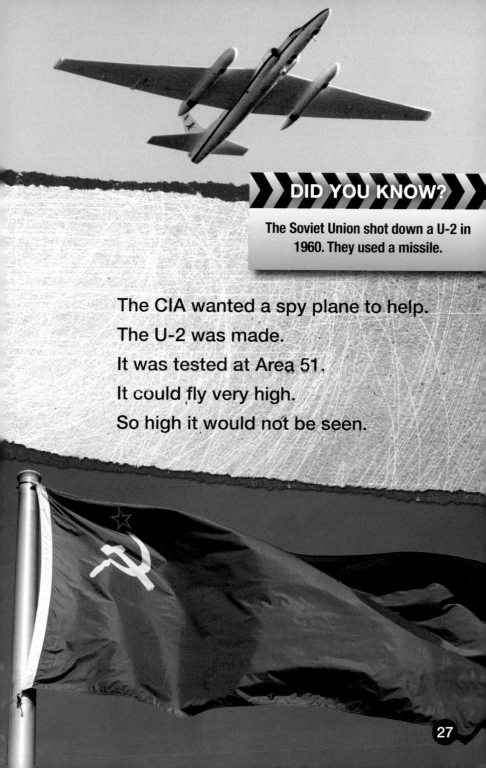

DID YOU KNOW?

The Soviet Union shot down a U-2 in 1960. They used a missile.

The CIA wanted a spy plane to help.

The U-2 was made.

It was tested at Area 51.

It could fly very high.

So high it would not be seen.

A new plane came out in the 1960s.

The A-12 Oxcart.

It had a strange shape.

Part of it was wide.

Shaped like a disc.

It could fly very fast.

2,300 miles per hour.

It was tested at Area 51 too.

Other planes were tested in the 1970s.

Have Blue was one.

Tacit Blue was another.

Tacit Blue was shaped like a whale.

But it stayed hidden.

This made it a *stealth* plane.

Chapter 6
MORE SECRET PROJECTS

Spy planes.

We know about some of them.

Those used in the past.

But not today.

The military is always making new models.

They want them faster.

More quiet.

Harder to find.

And they must keep them secret.

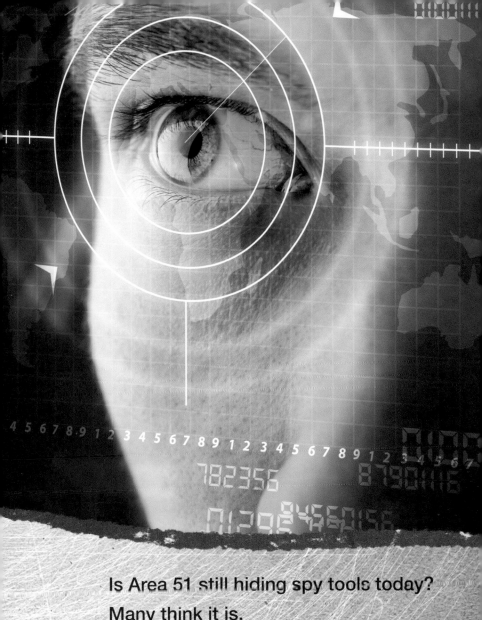

Is Area 51 still hiding spy tools today?

Many think it is.

We can't know.

But there are *rumors*.

Ideas of new secret projects.

Drones are one of them.

The military likes drones.

They have no pilot.

No one to be shot down with a plane.

What about space planes?
Some think they are being tested.
Area 51 would be a good place to do it.

We know about stealth planes.
What about helicopters?
Stealth copters.
If they exist, they may be at Area 51.

Chapter 7
ALIEN SECRETS?

Area 51 has many secrets.
Are there more than spy planes there?
Some think so.
They tell stories.
Stories about aliens.

Some wonder about the U.S. spy planes.
How did the military design them?
What made the planes so fast?

Some say it is alien *technology*.

They say there are spaceships at Area 51.
From other planets.

Photos show Area 51 buildings.
But many think there is more there.
Underground.
Secret floors.

Movies have shown this idea.
So have TV shows.
Secret labs.
Captured aliens.
Captured alien ships.
Is any of it true?
No one knows.

UNDERGROUND HALLWAYS

DID YOU KNOW?

A movie came out in 1996.
Independence Day. It showed secret
levels of Area 51. A captured alien
and a spaceship were there.

Chapter 8
LAZAR'S STORY

A man made big news in 1989.
His name was Robert Lazar.
He said he worked at Area 51.
He said he had seen alien
ships there.
Nine of them.
Captured by the U.S. military.

Lazar went on TV.
He said he worked on the ships.
He said he found a power source.
It could be used for U.S. planes.
People were shocked.
Could this be true?

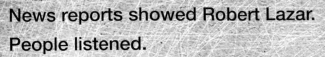

News reports showed Robert Lazar.
People listened.
They started talking about UFOs.

Some looked closer.
They checked out his story.
They said Robert Lazar was a liar.
He lied about where he went
to school.
The Air Force said he never worked
at Area 51.

Lazar said he was telling the truth.
He said people didn't want him to.
So they made it look like he was lying.

DID YOU KNOW?

Lazar called the power source he found on the spaceship "Element 115." He said it was rusty and heavy.

Today, Lazar won't talk.

He says he has nothing to do with UFOs.

But people still wonder.

Was he telling the truth in 1989?

Or just trying to get on TV?

Chapter 9
SPACESHIPS OR SPY PLANES?

Many people tell stories.

They say they saw a UFO.

Some say they saw aliens too.

Some of these stories are from Area 51.

People driving nearby.

Or stopped on the side of the road.

The stories mention strange shapes.

Weird lights.

Fast-moving aircraft.

That's why they think it is alien.

But is it?

DID YOU KNOW?

Robert Lazar said there was a good spot to watch spaceships take test flights. It was a mailbox on Nevada Highway 375. A black mailbox. It belongs to a local rancher. The rancher has now painted it white.

Area 51 was a test site.
Spy planes took off.
Flew overhead.
Some had strange shapes.
Some were shaped like discs.
They were all very fast.

The tests were secret.
Some were done at night.
People may have seen one.
They may have thought it
was a UFO.

Chapter 10
STILL A MYSTERY

Area 51 is a real place.

It is on maps now.

And we know planes were

tested there.

Spy planes.

But it is still a *mystery* too.

Guards patrol it.

Signs warn people away.

One president signed an order.

It said Area 51 was exempt.

Test results could be kept secret.

AREA 51

DO NOT
ENTER

Secrets always make
people wonder.
What else is hiding at Area 51?
It may not be aliens.
But there are secret projects.
Military projects.

Some day we will know.
But not today.

GLOSSARY

alien: a living being from outer space

disc: a thin and flat circular object

enemy: a nation that acts against another nation

experiment: a test to find out something new

hangar: a wide shed used to house airplanes

military: the armed forces of a nation

mystery: anything that is kept secret or remains unknown

nuclear weapon: a bomb that explodes with great force and energy

oath: a formal promise

rumor: a story that is not based on facts

satellite: a machine that orbits the earth

sensor: a device that reacts to light or movement and can send out a signal

sighting: something unusual that is seen by a person

standoff: a tie with no clear winner

static: jumbled sounds on a radio due to electricity

stealth: aircraft difficult to detect by sight, sound, or radar

technology: electronic or machine-based inventions

trespassing: going uninvited onto land that does not belong to you

UFO: an unexplained moving object in the sky; unidentified flying object

unmarked: no sign or words to show where something came from

TAKE A LOOK INSIDE

DRONES

Chapter 3
WORKING FOR US

Drones have a lot of uses.
They go where we cannot.

They see inside volcanoes.
Spy for us in war.
Save wild animals.
Find lost hikers.
Track wildfires.
Watch storms.
Dive into the ocean.

14

15

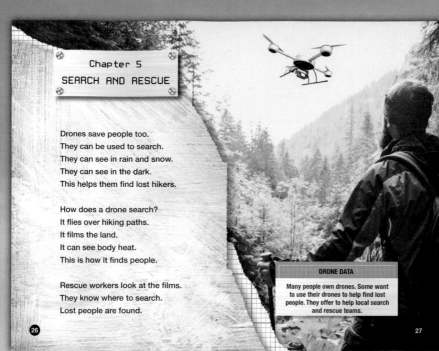

Chapter 5
SEARCH AND RESCUE

Drones save people too.
They can be used to search.
They can see in rain and snow.
They can see in the dark.
This helps them find lost hikers.

How does a drone search?
It flies over hiking paths.
It films the land.
It can see body heat.
This is how it finds people.

Rescue workers look at the films.
They know where to search.
Lost people are found.

DRONE DATA

Many people own drones. Some want to use their drones to help find lost people. They offer to help local search and rescue teams.

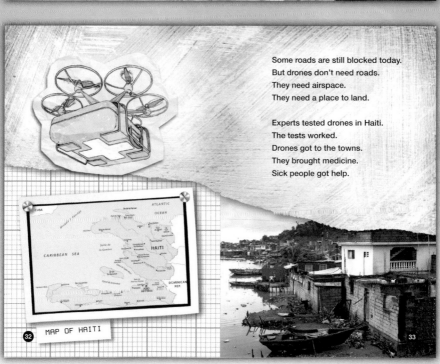

Some roads are still blocked today.
But drones don't need roads.
They need airspace.
They need a place to land.

Experts tested drones in Haiti.
The tests worked.
Drones got to the towns.
They brought medicine.
Sick people got help.

MAP OF HAITI

red rhino
bOOks®

NONFICTION

9781680210293

9781680210286

9781680210309

9781680210330

9781680210361

9781680210323

9781680210316

9781680210538

9781680210347

9781680210354